Oliver and the Eucalyptus Tree

Leanne Murner

Illustrated by Kat Fox

For more books in this collection visit 5littlebears.com.au

Serenity Press Pty Ltd
Waikiki, WA 6169

First published by Serenity Press (Serenity Press Kids) in 2021
www.serenitypress.org

National Library of Australia
Cataloguing in-Publication entry

Murner, Leanne (Leanne, Murner), Oliver and the Eucalyptus Tree

ISBN: 978-0-6453559-0-1 (hc)
ISBN: 978-0-6453559-1-8 (e)

Oliver and the Eucalyptus Tree

Leanne Murner

Illustrated by Kat Fox

"How are you going back there, Oliver, did you want to stop for a drink?" asked Poppy John.

"Yes," said Oliver.

"Okay, let's stop here and have a break." said Poppy.

"What is this tree, Poppy? It's huge!" said Oliver.

"This is a eucalyptus tree," said Poppy.

"What is all these squiggly lines on the tree, did someone carve into it?" said Oliver.

"These squiggly lines are caused by the grub of the scribbly gum moth," said Poppy.

"So how does it make all these lines, Poppy?" said Oliver.

"The moth lays its larvae under the bark and when the grub hatches, it travels under the bark, feeding on the tree and all these marks it has made in its path."

"Where are all those ants going, Poppy?" said Oliver.

"These are white ants, or you might know them as termites. They will be heading up the tree to that big nest. These termites eat the dead inner flesh of the tree, causing some eucalyptus trees to become hollow," said Poppy.

"So, will the tree then die if they eat it all away?" said Oliver.

"The termites start feeding on the inner wood, this timber is dead already, and easy for them to eat. These trees can survive being hollow, and when the tree becomes hollow it creates homes for animals and birds to live in. This can be called pipe nesting. The wildlife living in the tree will then drop food scraps, droppings and seed backlog inside the hollow of the tree that then is turned into a fertiliser for the tree." said Poppy.

"Oh, Poppy, I can see some heads popping out of the termite nest," said Oliver.

"That will be baby kookaburras. The adult kookaburra will make a hole in the side of the termite nest and lay their eggs. Once the eggs hatch into chicks, the thick walls of the termite nest will help keep the babies warm until they are big enough to fly. Once the birds leave the nest the termites will then repair the hole," said Poppy.

"Have a look up there in the treetops through the binoculars, can you see anything else?" asked Poppy John.

"Yes, Poppy, I can see a koala, it is eating some leaves," said Oliver.

"Koalas only eat eucalyptus leaves. They are very picky with their food, so only eat the leaves from certain types of eucalyptus. The koala will sleep for around 18 to 22 hours a day in the tree because these leaves do not provide much energy for them," said Poppy.

"Here, Oliver, can you smell these leaves? They have a very strong smell. Did you know that there are heaps of uses for the eucalyptus leaves? They can be made into herbal teas to treat colds and flu, or processed into an oil for herbal use," said Poppy John.

"Oh, Poppy, can I take some home to show mum and dad?" said Oliver.

"Yes, of course," said Poppy.

"What else can you see up in the treetops?" said Poppy John.

"I can see some white cockatoos eating the blossoms and there is some little bees there, too. I thought flowers only came out over spring and summer?" said Oliver.

"Plants flower over both warm and cold months, this helps to provide food for birds and insects and help with cross-pollination of the plants that need to survive all year round. If plants did not flower over the colder months, the birds and bees would not have anything to eat. This is a very important element in nature for the birds and insects to survive and help to pollinate other plants so they can grow," said Poppy John.

"Shhhh, do not move, there is an echidna heading our way, we don't want to scare it off," said Poppy. "It must be on the hunt for some food. Echidnas eat ants, beetles, worms, and moth larvae. They are drawn to these trees because of the termites. They like to scratch around in the leaf litter on the ground looking for insects," said Poppy.

"Oh, Poppy, what is it doing?" asked Oliver.

"We must have scared it, it has curled into a ball and is quickly digging a shallow hole, so that only its sharp spines are exposed. They do this to protect themselves from predators. Let's keep going, Oliver, so we do not disturb it," said Poppy.

"Why is all this bark peeling off the tree?" said Oliver.

"As the bark dries and peels, it helps keep the tree healthy. As the tree sheds its bark, it also sheds any mosses, fungi and parasites that may live on the bark. When it falls to the ground, it creates homes for small reptiles and insects. This will also create a ground cover to protect the soil from the heat in the warmer months," said Poppy John.

"See here, Oliver, this is a branch from a eucalyptus. It has been hollowed out by termites," said Poppy. "Branches like these are used by the Aboriginals to make their musical instruments, like the didgeridoo and clap sticks, or digging and hunting tools."

"These hollow branches on the ground are also creating homes for small reptiles. See here, Oliver, this is the home for this little lizard and a frog, so we better put it down, we don't want to disturb them," said Poppy.

"Oh, look over here, Oliver," said Poppy. "This is a little microbat, they like to live in hollow trees but they will also hide in small crevices on the outside of the tree and they like to feed on the insects that live there. The microbat will sleep all day and feed all night."

"It is so small, Poppy, it looks so cute! It is amazing how many animals and insects that live on the eucalyptus tree," said Oliver.

"What a great bush walk today," said Poppy.

"I cannot wait to tell mum and dad all about the eucalyptus tree and the animals we have seen!" said Oliver.

Eucalyptus Tree/Koala

These trees grow to great height and age, their bark and leaves differ over 700 species. The oil from the leaves is used in medicines and for aromatic purposes.

Flowers vary with each species, they are high in nectar and a food source for nectar birds, pollinators and insects.

Koalas survive on a diet of eucalyptus leaves and can eat up to a kilogram a day! Pretty impressive, considering eucalyptus is poisonous to most animals.

Koalas are quite picky eaters, eating less than 50 of the 700 eucalyptus species.

Koalas can sleep up to 18 hours a day because their bodies need a lot of energy to digest the gum leaves and when they are sleeping.

Sadly, koala numbers are on the decline. Their numbers have been falling further and further every year due to deforestation, fire and disease. This struggling species have now been pushed even further towards the brink of extinction.

Sugarbag Bee

These bees are small (about 3-5 mm in length), compact, dark-coloured bees. Each nest has a queen, drones and thousands of workers. These bees produce sugarbag honey, a highly prized food of Aboriginals who gathered it from wild nests. Each hive produces only small amounts of sugarbag, less than 1kg per year, and so it is a special product, to be savoured and relished.

Sugarbag bee nests are made of wax and resin, and are built in hollow tree trunks, branches, fallen logs and rock crevices. Unlike honey bees, the cells used to rear the larvae, the brood comb, are separated from larger 'pots' that are used to store the honey and pollen to feed.

Echidna

These prickly little guys evolved between 20 and 50 million years ago. This species is a unique, egg-laying mammal – one of just 3 in the world – and can live up to 45 years! Echidnas have toothless jaws, so to eat they put their slender snouts and strong claws to work, tearing open logs, ant hills and other food sources, then use their long sticky tongues (we're talking 15cm long!) and pads on the roof of their mouth to break down their food. They love nothing more than a meal of ants, termites, worms and insect larvae – and have been known to eat roughly 40,000 per day!

Did you know that echidnas are referred to as 'ecosystem engineers'? While they are not the most active of animals, they spend an incredible amount of time digging and moving up to 200 cubic metres of soil each year. This improves soil mixing and water penetration, reduces run-off and erosion, and ultimately makes for healthier soils, which can lead to plant growth.

Scribbly Gum Moth

Scribbly gums are spectacular Australian eucalyptus that get their name from the strange 'scribbles' left behind on their smooth bark. These zigzag tracks are tunnels made by the larvae of the scribbly gum moth and tell a story of the insect's life cycle. The female scribbly gum moth lays eggs between layers of old and new bark. The larvae burrow into the new bark, and as the old bark falls away, the feeding trails of the larva are revealed. The diameter of the tunnels increase as the larvae grow. When the larvae have reached their maximum size, they emerge and crawl out from between the bark and into the litter, or into cracks in the bark, where they form a elongated ridged grey cocoon. Adults emerge in the following autumn.

Kookaburra

Although kookaburras are known for being an Australian bird, only the blue-winged and laughing kookaburras are found in Australia. The other two species are also found in New Guinea.

Kookaburras are carnivorous and will eat insects, small mammals, lizards and even venomous snakes.

Kookaburras perch on branches and wait for their prey to approach. When the prey is in range, they swoop down and grab it in their big beaks

The kookaburras' laugh is a familiar sound in Australian woodlands and forests. It is used to mark and protect the birds' territory. Groups of kookaburras often start laughing at the same time, making an unforgettable din!

Microbat

Microbats see with their ears rather than their eyes. They produce a sound and listen for it as it bounces back from surrounding objects. When cruising, microbats emit about 10 pulses per second. When an insect is detected, the pulses go up to over 100 per second.

During summer and autumn, microbats go into a feeding frenzy as they fatten up on insects to help them survive the winter. Adult microbats feed on lawn grub moths, weevils, caterpillars, beetles, midges, flying termites, mosquitoes and other insects. Microbats can eat as much as 40% of their own body weight in a single night or several hundred insects per hour.

If these tiny bats cannot find a suitable hollow, they can fit into very small gaps and utilise your roof and walls. This is why artificial roost sites are important as they provide an alternative.

Dedication

I would like to dedicate this book to my best friend and husband. Thank you for supporting me through this amazing journey.

My Oliver for being my inspiration, Poppy John for his wealth of knowledge and support.

And to my amazing friend Amy for pushing me out of my comfort zone two years ago, starting my new life purpose.

I would not be here today without you believing in me.

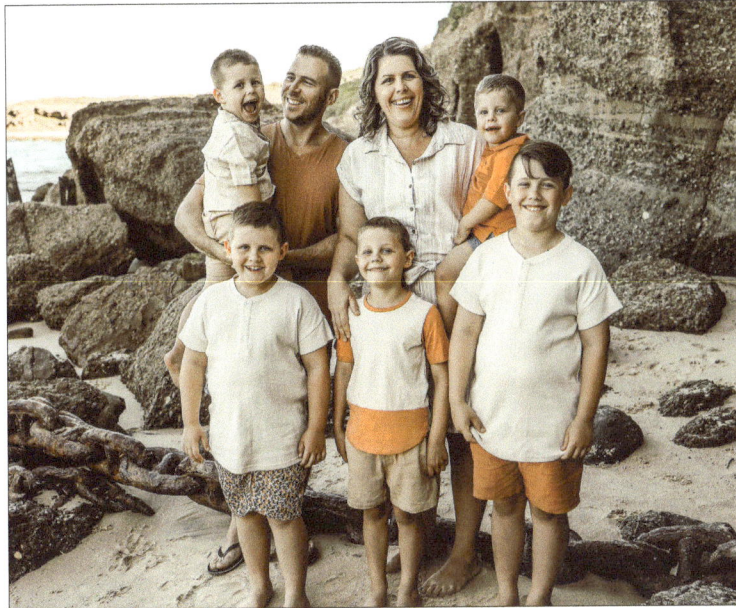

About the Author

Leanne Murner is an author, business owner/designer at 5 Little Bears Pty Ltd and a proud mum of five boys. Leanne saw a gap in the market for Australian themed wooden toys and began creating products for children with an educational and Australian twist. Being a creative soul Leanne grew the business fast and as time went by her product portfolio increased. In addition she has also published the first two of a series of six children's books, Franki and the Banskia, and Loui and the Grass Tree, with the remaining being published this year. Leanne wanted to teach kids about Australian native flora and fauna, what they are and who needs them to survive. Leanne is busy working on another series of books teaching kids about Australian animals and their habitat, threats and how we can help. Leanne is passionate that our children need to be better educated on Australian wildlife to help keep it from extinction.

www.ingramcontent.com/pod-product-compliance
Lightning Source LLC
Chambersburg PA
CBHW042024090426
42811CB00016B/1725